First World War
and Army of Occupation
War Diary
France, Belgium and Germany

30 DIVISION
Divisional Troops
Divisional Cyclist Company
7 November 1915 - 22 May 1916

WO95/2321/2

The Naval & Military Press Ltd
www.nmarchive.com
Published in association with The National Archives

Published by

The Naval & Military Press Ltd

Unit 10 Ridgewood Industrial Park,

Uckfield, East Sussex,

TN22 5QE England

Tel: +44 (0) 1825 749494

www.naval-military-press.com

www.nmarchive.com

This diary has been reprinted in facsimile from the original. Any imperfections are inevitably reproduced and the quality may fall short of modern type and cartographic standards.

© **Crown Copyright**
Images reproduced by permission of The National Archives, London, England, 2015.

Contents

Document type	Place/Title	Date From	Date To
Heading	WO95/2321/2 Nov 1915-May 1916 30th Divl. Cyclist Coy		
Heading	30th Division Divl Troops 30th Divl Cyclist Coy Nov 1915-May 1916		
Heading	30th Divl: Cyclist Vol: I 121/7708 No 15-May 16		
Heading	War Diary of 30th Divisional Cyclist Coy From 7th November 1915. To 30th. November, 1915. Volume I.		
War Diary		07/11/1915	19/11/1915
War Diary	Flesselles.	19/12/1915	28/12/1915
War Diary	Fienvillers.	29/12/1915	29/12/1915
Heading	30th Divl: Cyclist Vol 2 121/7936		
Heading	War Diary of 30th Divisional Cyclist Coy From The 1st December, 1915 To The 3rd December, 1915. Volume 2		
War Diary	Fienvillers.	01/12/1915	06/12/1915
War Diary	Outrebois	07/12/1915	27/12/1915
Heading	30th Div Cyclists Corrigenda to Vol I		
Miscellaneous	To O.C. No. 1 Platoon 30th D.C.C. Fienvillers From Cpl E. Webster	04/12/1915	04/12/1915
Miscellaneous	O.M.12 To O.C. No. 1 Platoon 30th Div Cyclist Co Fienvillers.	04/12/1915	04/12/1915
War Diary	O.M.12 To O.C. No. 1 Platoon 30th Div Cyclist Co Fienvillers.	04/12/1915	04/12/1915
Miscellaneous	To O.C. No. 1 Platoon 30th D.C.C. Fienvillers.	04/12/1915	04/12/1915
Miscellaneous	OC A Platoon 30th Div Cycling Corps	02/12/1915	02/12/1915
Miscellaneous	Fri Dec 3rd 1915 To OC 4 Platoon 30th Div Cycle Corp	03/12/1915	03/12/1915
Miscellaneous	Wed Dec 1st 1915 To O.C 1 Platoon 30th Div Cycle Corp	01/12/1915	01/12/1915
Miscellaneous	To O.C. 1 Platoon 30th Div Cyclist. Coy Dec 1/12/15	01/12/1915	01/12/1915
Miscellaneous	To O.C. A Platoon 30 D.C.C. Feinvillers.		
Miscellaneous	To O.C. 1 Platoon 30th Div Coy Cps	14/12/1915	14/12/1915
Miscellaneous	To O.C. 1 Platoon 30th Div Cy Cps Feinvillers.	04/12/1915	04/12/1915
Miscellaneous	To O.C. 1 Platoon. 30 Div Cy Cps. Feinvillers	04/12/1915	04/12/1915
Miscellaneous	To O.C. A Platoon. 30th Div. C.C.	02/12/1915	02/12/1915
Miscellaneous	To O.C. A Platoon. 30th D.C.C.	03/12/1915	03/12/1915
Miscellaneous	To O.C. 30th Div C. Corps. No 1 Platoon		
Miscellaneous	To O.C. No 1 Platoon 30th Div C. Corps.		
Miscellaneous	To O.C. A Platoon 30th Div Cycle Corps Directing Artillery.	03/12/1915	03/12/1915
Miscellaneous			
Miscellaneous	Ref Map OM 12. O.C. A Platoon 30 Div C Corp.	04/12/1915	04/12/1915
Miscellaneous	O.C. 1 Platoon 30th Divn. C.C. Ref Map A.M. 12. Dec 4th 1915	04/12/1915	04/12/1915
Miscellaneous	G.O.C. 30th Division.	04/12/1915	04/12/1915
Miscellaneous		03/12/1915	03/12/1915
Miscellaneous	From O.C. 30th Divisional Cyclist Coy	18/12/1915	18/12/1915
Diagram etc	Rough Sketch Of Route Taken By Div Artillery And Billeting Area.		
Heading	30 Div Cyclist Coy Vol.3		

Heading	War Diary. of 30th Divisional Cyclist Coy. From 1st January 1916 To 31st January 1916 Volume 3		
War Diary		01/01/1916	29/01/1916
Miscellaneous	Supplement to December, 1915		
Heading	30th Divl. Cyclist Vol 4		
Heading	War Diary Of 30th Divisional Cyclist Coy. From 1st February 1916 To 29th February 1916 Volume 4		
War Diary	Etinehem	01/02/1916	28/02/1916
War Diary			
Heading	War Diary of 30th Divisional Cyclist Coy. From 1st March, 1916 To 31st March, 1916 Volume 5		
War Diary		01/03/1916	29/03/1916
War Diary			
Heading	War Diary of 30th Divisional Cyclist Coy From 1st April, 1916 To 30th April 1916 Volume 6		
War Diary		02/04/1916	28/04/1916
Heading	War Diary of 30th Divisional Cyclist Coy From 1st May, 1916 To 22nd May 1916 Volume 7		
War Diary		01/05/1916	22/05/1916

WO 95
2321/2
Nov 1915 — May 1916
30TH DIVL. CYCLIST COY

30TH DIVISION
DIVL TROOPS

30TH DIVL CYCLIST COY.
NOV 1915 - MAY 1916

30th Sep: G club
Vol: I

12/7708

Nov 15
|
Mar 16

Confidential

War Diary

of

30th Divisional Cyclist Coy.

from 7th November, 1915. to 30th November, 1915.

Volume I.

Page 1.

Army Form C. 2118.

WAR DIARY
or
INTELLIGENCE SUMMARY.

(Erase heading not required.)

30th Divisional Cyclist Coy.

Hour, Date, Place.	Summary of Events and Information	Remarks and references to Appendices
1915. November 7th 12·0 Noon.	The Company entrained at AMESBURY, SALISBURY PLAIN, completely equipped. Strength:- Officer Commanding. Captain M.H.R. Paley. A Platoon Lieut G.W. Sons. " " W.F. Clarke. B 2nd " G.F. Ward. C 2nd " G. Grant. D 2nd " F.S. Scrutton. E 2nd " P.H. Browne. F 2nd " F.W. Lee. Other ranks 193. Total 201. 3 Horses.	MAP USED SET B. SHEET 12 AMIENS SCALE 1:80,000 Geographical Section, General Staff No 2526.
November 8th 5·0 pm	Embarked at Southampton on A.S.S. "Lydia".	
7·0 am	Disembarked at Havre at and proceeded to rest camp No 5. for the day	
8·0 pm	Entrained at Point No 4. Railway siding Havre station.	
12·0 mn	Left Havre.	
November 9th 11·0 am	Detrained at PONT REMY, SOMME and marched into billets	
1·0 pm	at VILLERS - SOUS - AILLY. arriving without casualties.	

Page 2

Army Form C. 2118.

Instructions regarding War Diaries and Intelligence
Summaries are contained in F.S. Regs., Part II
and the Staff Manual respectively. Title pages
will be prepared in manuscript.

WAR DIARY
or
INTELLIGENCE SUMMARY.
(Erase heading not required.)

30th Divisional Cyclist Coy.

Hour, Date, Place		Summary of Events and Information	Remarks and references to Appendices
1915 November. 10th		A Platoon detailed for duty at Divisional Headquarters at AILLY-LE-HAUT CLOCHER	Duties - Guards.
		The billeting accommodation at VILLERS SOUS AILLY was very poor. Sanitary arrangements needed very careful supervision. Water supply good, but owing to valant elevators being in use the greatest care was necessary in the drawing.	
" 18th	11.0 am	The Company left VILLERS SOUS AILLY and marched into billets at	
	2.30 pm	FLESSELLES (VIA FLIXECOURT and VIGNACOURT)	
" 19th		Letter received as follows:-	
		"Officer Commanding	
		30th Divisional Cyclist Coy.	
		The G.O.C. was pleased to notice the smart appearance of your men on the march to-day.	
		He specially noticed how well their clothing, equipment and rifles were turned out."	
		signed L Holland Major	
		General Staff	
		30th Division	
		18th November 1915.	

Page. 3

Army Form C. 2118.

Instructions regarding War Diaries and Intelligence Summaries are contained in F.S. Regs., Part II. and the Staff Manual respectively. Title pages will be prepared in manuscript.

WAR DIARY
or
INTELLIGENCE SUMMARY.
(Erase heading not required.)

30th Divisional Cyclist Coy.

Hour, Date, Place	Summary of Events and Information	Remarks and references to Appendices
1915 December 19th. FLESSELLES.	The Platoon on duty at Headquarters (70th) having completed their period of duty were this day relieved by No. 6 Platoon.	
" 21st.	Orders received for 1 Sgt. 1 Cpl. & 6 men to report to the E.A.P. APM. for espionage 'C' duty. These 8 men were attached to Headquarters. Also 7 men to be attached to the Signal Coy R.E. as short distance messengers. Also 5 men to be attached to Headquarters on general fatigue duty	
" 28th	The Billeting accommodation at FLESSELLES was found to be very poor indeed. The shortage of water, all of which was rain water, gathered into wells and of a poor quality caused considerable trouble. This day the Company moved by road to FIENVILLERS. The day was fine and clear. A hard frost causing the road surface to be in good condition for cycling.	
9.15 am	Left FLESSELLES	
11.5 am	Arrived at FIENVILLERS. The Billeting accommodation at FIENVILLERS was an improvement on FLESSELLES Water supply ample. A room was set apart for bathing purposes and the whole Company were able to enjoy a good hot bath.	

...... Captain,
Commanding 30th Divisional Cyclist Coy.

Page 4.

Army Form C. 2118.

WAR DIARY
or
INTELLIGENCE SUMMARY.

(Erase heading not required.)

30th Divisional Cyclist Coy.

Hour, Date, Place	Summary of Events and Information	Remarks and references to Appendices
		MAP USED. SET B. SHEET 12. AMIENS. SCALE 1: 80.000 Geographical Section. General Staff No 2526.
1915. December. 29th. FIENVILLERS.	Orders received for 1 officer & 12 men to report to R.T.O DOULLENS to act as guides to the incoming Artillery &c. Lieut W.T CLARKE and 12 men of No A Platoon detailed, and duly proceeded to DOULLENS.	

M.M.Paley..........CAPTAIN,
COMMANDING 30TH DIVISIONAL CYCLIST COY.

30th Intl. Cyclists
vol. 2

121/7936

Confidential
War Diary
of
30th Divisional Cyclist Coy.
from the 1st December, 1915 to the 31st December, 1915.
Volume 2.

WAR DIARY
INTELLIGENCE SUMMARY

Army Form C. 2118

Page 5

30th Divisional Cyclist Coy

Hour, Date, Place	Summary of Events and Information	Remarks and references to Appendices
1915 December 1st FIENVILLERS	The Platoon on duty at Divisional Headquarters, No C. were this day relieved by No E Platoon.	
" 2nd	Orders received from D.H.Q. to detail 50 men exclusive of N.C.Os to report to the R.T.O. at Doullens for fatigue work in connection with the detraining of Artillery. This work was accomplished on the 4th inst.	
" 6th	The following letter received :- O.C. 30th Divisional Cyclist Coy. The S.O.C. desires to express his appreciation of the excellent manner in which Lieutenant Clarke and the party of Cyclist Guides, detailed to escort the Artillery from Railhead to their billeting area carried out their duties. Signed L Hume-Spry Lieut-Colonel A.A. & Q.M.G. 30th Division 6-12-1915. Orders received to move the whole Company early on the 7th to OUTREBOIS	

PAGE 6.

WAR DIARY
or
INTELLIGENCE SUMMARY.
(Erase heading not required.)

Army Form C.

30th Divisional Cyclist Coy.

Hour, Date, Place		Summary of Events and Information	Remarks and references to Appendices
1915 December	7th OUTREBOIS	The Company left FIENVILLERS at 9·0 AM by road for OUTREBOIS and arrived at 10 AM	
"	13th "	The Platoon on duty at Divisional Headquarters, No 6 Platoon were this day relieved by No 7 Platoon.	
"	20th "	7 Platoon at D.H.Q. relieved by No 9 Platoon.	
"	27th "	1 Officer & 21 O.R. proceeded to LONGUEVILLETTE to undergo a course of instruction in Bombing.	
		The following additions to the Mobilization Store Table A.F. O.1098/122	
		Spades G.S. mainly for sanitary work — 6	
		— do — 3	
		Axes pick — do —	
		Tools carpenters for repairing bounds &c for billets have been loaned to us from Divisional Stores by the R.E.	
		A Motor cycle for the use of the S.O. is very essential. To be able to visit all points on an extended scheme as nearly as possible

PAGE 7

WAR DIARY
or
INTELLIGENCE SUMMARY.

Army Form ...
No. 2118...
Date 31/1/19/15
30th Divisional Cyclist Coy

Hour, Date, Place	Summary of Events and Information	Remarks and references to Appendices

the same time is not only conducive to greater discipline and close attention to detailed instructions by subordinate ranks but enables the C.O. to explain in fuller detail the improvements that must take place in communication and report work, after visiting the whole scheme at almost a given time.

Also a Divisional Cyclist Coy is divided into parties for various duties ie. Divisional Head Quarters. Bombing Guides. Provost &c. and to enable the C.O. to frequently visit each of the parties a motor cycle is necessary.

30 li stri: Eçalate
Crisjaula 6 Vol I

II.   Dec 4th 1915.

To O.C. No 1 Platoon
30th D.C.C. Fienvillers

Ref: M4
C.19.12.   From Cpl E. Webster

Report No 3 Guiding Artillery Dec 3rd left DOULLENS at 7-35 AM for ST. OUEN with No 151 B.A.C. Reached destination at 1 P.M.

Travelling. Through the continual rain the roads became very heavy after the first journey. Considering the state of the roads & the tired condition of the horses things went very well. Only had one or two cases of waggons being stuck and these occurred on the rise passing through HEM.

                                Cpl. E. Webster.

30 Div Cyclists
December 1915

U.M.17
To O.C.
N° 1 Platoon
30th Div Cyclist Co
FIENVILLERS.

Report N° 2.

Acted as guide to 150th Brigade
D Battery and 1/5th DAC 1 Section
left DOULLENS at 12.15 A.M
2nd Decr. Halted at HEM for
½ hour to water horses. Halted
at FIENVILLERS for 20 minutes
and again at DOMART for 20
minutes. Arrived BERTEAUCOURT
lès DAMES at 5.30 P.M handed
Column over to billeting officers.
Arrived DOULLENS on return
journey 5.30 A.M 3rd December/15

FIENVILLERS
Dec 4/15

Stanley A Smethurst
N° 9083.
Cyclist

A.M. 12.
To O.C.
  No. 1 Platoon
  10th Divisional Cyclist Co.
    FIENVILLERS.

Report No. 1.

Acted as guide to 148th
Brigade Battery Artillery. Left
DOULLENS Station at 2.15 A.M
1st Decr 1915. Halted at DOULLENS
Railway Crossing for half an hour
as the column was cut through
by team. Went through to
ST LEGER arriving there at
6.45 AM where the O.C. dismissed
me. Arrived DOULLENS on
return journey at 4 p.m. 1st Decr
1915.

              Stanley Broadhead
FIENVILLERS   No 9083.
Decr 4th 1915   Cyclist

O.M. 12
To O.C.
No. 1 Platoon
30 Div: C.C.
Fienvillers

4/12/15

Report No 1
Guiding
Artillery

Left DOULLENS at 10 p.m. 30/11/15 in charge of 148 Brig. Ammunition Column, halted on Hill between HEM and HARDIVAL, then straight to ST. LEGER, arrived 5-30 a.m 1/12/15, could find no one to take charge, left them with C C B. Battery, reported back to DOULLENS at 8-15 a.m 1/12/15.

Report No 2 Left DOULLENS at 8-40 a.m 2/12/15 in charge of 150 Brig: C Battery halted at FIENVILLERS 2 hours food and water, horses, arrived at BERTEAUCOURT-LES-DAMES at 3-15 p.m 2/12/15 handed them over to an

Interpreter and O.C of A
Battery, reported back at
DOULLENS at 6-15 p.m.

9105 H.F. Brown
Cyclist

4/12/15
Hénuvillers

To O.C. N°1 Platoon   Dec 4th 1915
30th D.C.C. Fienvillers

Ref M.F.   From Cpl E. Webster
M.12.

Report N°1 Guiding Artillery. Nov 30th left DOULLENS at
6 P.M. for Bethencourt St Ouen with 149D
Battery, but after passing DOMART was met
by a Staff Officer who instructed me to take
the battery to PERNOIS. Reached latter place
at 9-30 PM and had a lot of trouble in
billeting. The Maire had not made any
arrangements and he passed us on to
a subordinate official who took us from
place to place finally accommodating
us at 11-30 p.m. I rested with the
battery until 6 A.M. Dec 1st and then returned to DOULLENS.

Report N°2 Guiding Artillery Dec 2nd left DOULLENS
at 2 A.M. for ST OUEN with D.A.C.
A + B Sub. Sects. of N°1 Section. Travelled
very well and reached destination at
8-30 A.M. Had breakfast then returned to
DOULLENS.

AM 12.

O.C. A Platoon
30th Div Cycling Corps
Friday Dec 2/15.

7·30 am left FIENVILLERS with party of Cyclists for DOULLENS to assist in unloading 30th Div Artillery luggage etc.

10 o'clock pm Acted as guide for 151 Coy B Battery from DOULLENS to BERTEAUCOURT. arrived BERTEAUCOURT 5 o'clock am Dec 3/15 nobody at Berteaucourt to receive the battery. at 5·30 am I was sent by the O.C. B Battery to ST OUEN with a message to the Adjutant of the 151 Coy A Battery asking him if he had any instructions re Billets for 151 Coy B Battery. he didn't know anything about the billets of B Battery - but sent a message back advising the C.O. B Battery to get

Fri Dec 3rd 1915
To A.C. & Platform
30th Div Cycl. Corp

Acted as Guide to
Hdqrs D.A.C.
Departure Left Doullens 3-30 a.m
picked up stranded waggon
a mile outside Herv-
Accident While getting waggon going
2 horses fell driver underneath
driver was got out & was not
seriously hurt a delay was caused
of about 2 hours in getting
moving again
Watering Horses Watered horses at Fienvillers
picked up several stranded
waggons canvas bucket rugs
waterproof sheets Etc & arrived
at St Ouen at 11-30 noon
Column was taken over by
a Sergt of Artillery
P.L. J Evans 9562
30th Div Cycl Corps

Wed Dec 1st 1915
To O.C 1 Platoon
30th Div Cycle Corp

Acted as Guide to 149th Brigade
1/3 Battery, Capt Gatenhill in command
Departure left Doulens 2-30 p.m., stopped
watering horses to water horses at Fienvillers
Accident Gun knocked down by gun carriage
& wrecked my machine continued
journey on horseback & arrived
Bernard 10-30 p.m.

Pte J Evans 4564
1 Platoon
30 Div Cycle Corp

To O.C. 1 platoon
30th Div Cyclist Coy
Dec 1/12/15

Report No 1
Guiding
Artillery

Taken charge of battery
D 149 at 9.45 A.M. horses
were watered at HEM.
Arrived at ST LEGER
5 P.M. Received by battery
billeting officer.

Report No 2
Guiding
Artillery

Taken charge of 150th
brigade Ammunition
column at 4.45 P.M.
Column was broken half
way between HEM, FIE
NVILLERS, G.S. waggon
left in ditch. Arrived at
BERTEAUCOURT
LES DAMES 12 M.N.
no one to receive column

Dec 4/15
Doullens

Pte J Stevson
1 platoon

To O.C. a Platoon 20 D.C.C.
          Feinvillers.

I was told off to guide to a Batt 149 Bdge
to PERNOIS. at 3-33 am Dec 1st. They
arrived at 10.30 a.m. and we moved off at
11.30 a.m. We halted at M. to water the horses
and after 4 halts we arrived at PERNOIS
at 7.30 p.m. There was no one there to receive
us. Having a puncture in my back tyre I stayed
the night at PERNOIS I left ~~Doullens~~
PERNOIS at 6 am Dec 2nd and arrived
at DOULLENS at 11-0 a.m. I was then
told that I was to take the a Batt
151 Bdge to ST. OUEN. We moved off
at 7.15 p.m. Dec 2nd after we had passed
through FEINVILLERS we found part
of the Divisional Ammunition Column
We told them to follow on in the rear
of my Batt. We arrived at ST. OUEN
at 2.30 am Dec 3rd. I then returned
to DOULLENS where I arrived at 10-0 am
I lost my pedal during the night

          Cyclist C.A. Mousley
               9079

To O.C.
1 Platoon "30th Div Cy Cps
Fienvillers

3.

On Dec 3rd.15. I acted again as guide to "D" Batt of the 151 Bry from Doullens to St Ouen. We started at 9 a.m. & went on through Hem on to Fienvilliers, where we halted to water & feed the Horses for 1hr viz 12oc to 1oc. Then we went on straight through to St Ouen, landing there at 5.30PM where after taking the Horses to their billets I was dismissed & asked if I'd like to wait & have some tea, in about an hour, but I came back to Fienvilliers, where we are billeted.

4/12/15

Merlin Eaton

66

To. O.C.
 1st Platoon   30th Div. Cy. Corps
         Terivillers.

No 1.
      On Nov 30th 1915. I acted as
guide to 'C' Batt. 149 Brig. to
Bethencourt, from Doullens & 12?:-

We left Doullens at. 11.55 + the
1st Halt was on the Road between
Doullens + Hem for the purpose
of Watering the Horses at the
River, L'Authie. the Watering lasted
3/4 of an hour, then from River we
went through Hem Hardinval. Terivillers.
Beauval. Domart. St Leger St Ouen
on to Bethencourt, where I handed
the Batt. over to the Billiting Officer
who accompanied us to billett the Men
We landed at Bethencourt at 4.30 PM
On arriving back to Doullens, I
found out the Batt. should have
gone to Pernois.
        4/12/15   Melvin Eaton.

67 To. OC
1 Platoon. 30 Div Cy 6/00.
Fienvillers

2

On Dec 1st I acted as guide to B Batt. 150 Brigade from Doullens Stat. to Berteaucourt. We started at 9.30 PM & went onto Hardinval where we halted for a breath. We lost on the way a few Horse Rugs &c & two Horses had the Cholic but they soon got round — we went straight through to Berteaucourt, where we landed at 4.30 AM. After handing the Batt. over to the Billetting Officer I was dismissed So slept in a Barn till 8.oc. then I returned to Doullen's for Breakfast.

4/12/15.

Merlin Eaton

No. 1 Journey

Dec 3/15.

To: O.C. H Platoon. 30th Div. C.C.

A.m. 12.   Director of Artillery

Left Doullens 6.30 P.M.
Guide 15 OA Battery.
Arrived Bertrancourt
12.30 A.M. Left them in
charge of the interpreter
at the Hotel de Ville.

Cyclist Dickinson
No 9081
Dec 4/15

73. A̲⁸ 12   Dec 3/15.
To 6.C. A Platoon. 30 S. C. C.
No Journey

Left Jouellens 5 P. M.
Guide 157 C. Battery
arrived St Ouen
12. A. M. Left them in
charge of a Sergeant-
major of another Battery
who had arrived
earlier

Cyclist Dickinson
no 9 081.
Dec 4/15 —

106

To O.C.
50th Aus. C. Corps.
N° 1 Platoon

Ref. Map. 2 in. 12
Second Dec 1915

Report N°2.   Guide to
~~Coy~~ D.A.C. ⅔ 8½
Lt. Sutherland Sutton

Left Doullens seven o'clock
in the morning for St Ouen
Stopped to feed and
water at Halm, arrived
St Ouen two thirty
in the afternoon. He was
recieved by a captain
of his own unit who
had all arrangements
for his men.

Doullens.
                          Cyclist
                          F. Harrington

To O.C.
    No 1 Platoon
    30th Div C. Corps
                Ref Map Sh 12
                Thirteen Nov. 1915
Report No 1.   Guide to
            No 148. B. Battery
            Capt Knowles &c

Left Doullens seven o'clock
at night for St Leger.
Arrived St Leger without
stopping at ~~2nd~~ eleven
o'clock at night. 2nd Lt
Zeigler who travelled
with us was left to do
all billeting arrangements.

            Cyclist
            T Warrington

Doullens.

... 1A   Dec 3/15

To OC A Platoon 30th Div Cycle Corps

            Divistag Artillery

Journey No 1

Left DOULLENS 7-0 AM
Wednesday Dec 1st -15 as
guide to 148 HQ & A Battery
arrived ST LEGER 1-10 pm
same date

Left OC of Battery (Col
Ormrod) in charge of OC
of another Battery which
had arrived previously at
that place.

Arrived back DOULLENS 4-30 pm.

74

Journey

Left DOULLENS 4-15 pM
Thursday Dec 2nd 1915 as
guide to 2/3 of the D.A.C.
in charge of Lieut Dalglish
arrived ST OUEN 12-15 A.M
Friday Dec 3rd 1915
 No one met the
column at ST OUEN but
I found the interpreter at
1-0 AM & left Lieut Dalglish
in his care.
 Arrived back DOULLENS 4-10AM

Ref map. D.M. 17.
O.C. A Platoon
 30 Div C Coy.

No 1
Guide to Dir A C. Capt Sinclair

Left Doullens at 1 am on
Dec 3. 1915. One waggon was
left behind under guard
1 mile from Doullens being
overturned in a ditch,
After leaving more waggons
stuck at different points
on the road we arrived
at St Ouen with the
remainder at 9 am.
The party was then taken
over by one of the men
of the R.F.A and shown
their billets.

Pte S.S. Knaggs.

Dec 4 1915
Franvillers

O.C. 1 Platoon
30th Div C.C.
Ref. Map S.F. 12
Dec. 4th 1915

Guide to B. Bailey
149 Ammn Column

Left Doullens 4.00 P.M. Dec. 1st for
Amiens. Delayed 45 minutes 1 mile S.W.
of Hem through wagons getting fast
in the Hill forpurched went to
Amiens arriving 9th. met there by one
of their own men and shown their
billets. handed over 9.30 by O.C. Ammn Column.

Cyclist S. Carter
1 Platoon
30 Div C.C.

Doullens

71

G.O.C.
30th DIVISION.

I have the honour to enclose
a report of the detraining
of The 30th Div ARTILLERY
at DOULLENS Nov 29th - Dec 3rd

ALSO Attached.
Rough sketch of Route taken
and ARTILLERY AREA (BILLETING)
Route marked in red.
Your Obedient Servant

W.F. Clarke Lt
30th Div Cyclist Co

4 Dec 1915

into touch with the Mayor of BERTEAUCOURT. I ask him to assist him in finding billets for B Battery. arrived back BERTEAUCOURT 6·30 am. proceeded to find Mayor of Berteaucourt & got into touch with him at 7 o'clock am. left the O.C. 181st Coy B Battery in charge of the Mayor & left Berteaucourt 7-18 a.m. for return journey to DOULLENS arriving 11 o'clock am. instructed to return to FIENVILLERS & report to Capt Says. left DOULLENS 12·30 am arrived FIENVILLERS 2·15 pm reported to Capt Says (per Lt Ward) 2·30 pm

J W Chapman L/Cpl
A Platson

Dec 3/15

From. O.C.
30th Divisional Cyclist Coy.

To The Officer
i/c Adjutant Generals Office
Base.

Subject:- War Diaries
Ref. War Diary 30th Divl Cyclist Coy.
7th Nov to 30th Nov 1915.

Will you be good enough to refer to the above Diary
Page 3
    We have in the first column   1915 December 19th.
    This should read.   1915 November 19th.
Page 4
        —"—   1915 December 29th
    should be   1915 November 29th

We regret the error and shall be glad if you
will kindly correct the same.

18-12-1915.   R. Patey, Captain
                                     Comd 30th Divl Cyclist Coy.

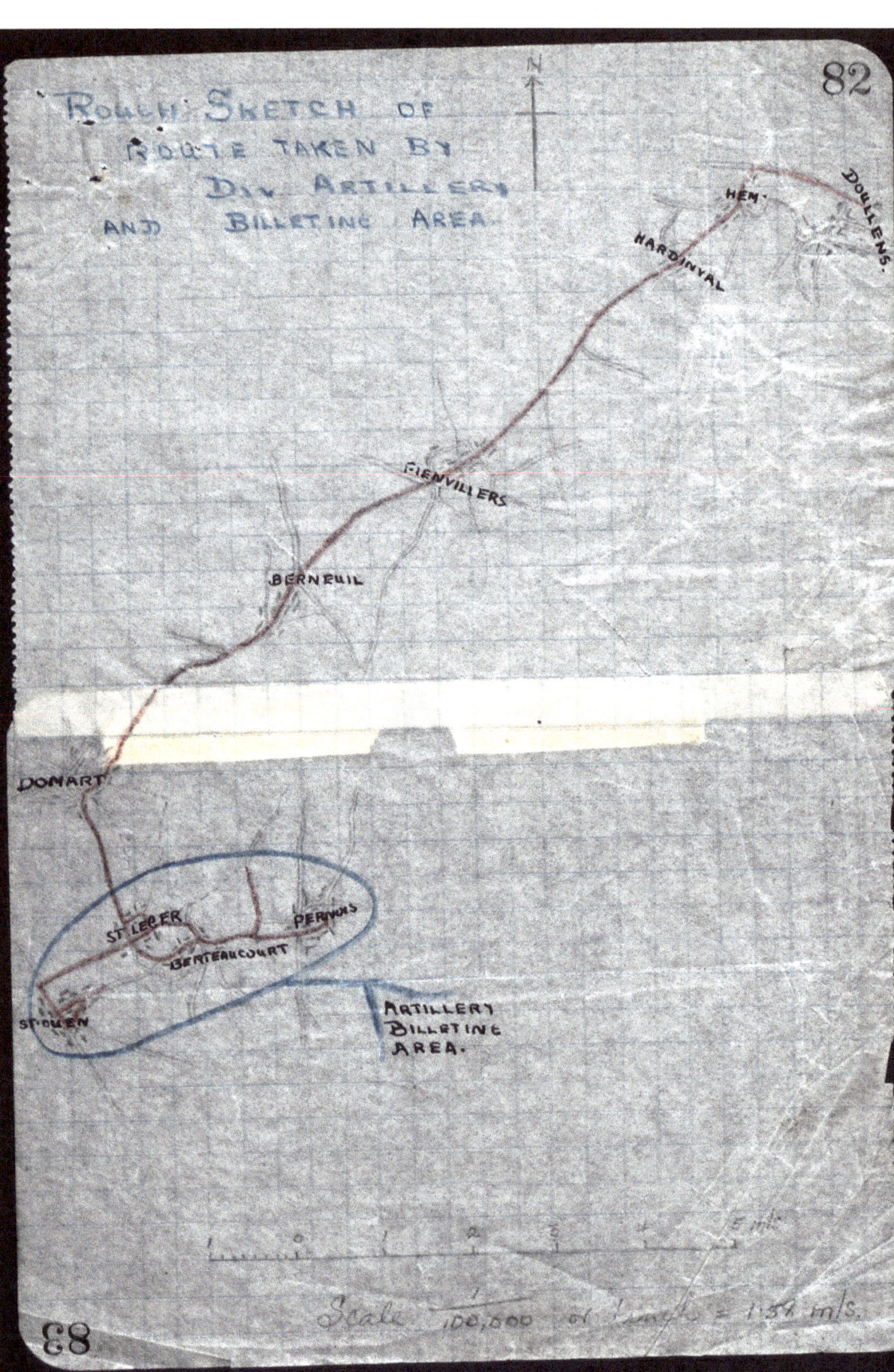

30 Div
Cyclist Coy
Vol. 3

Confidential

War Diary.

of

30th Divisional Cyclist Coy.

from 1st January 1916 to 31st January 1916

Volume 3.

WAR DIARY
or
INTELLIGENCE SUMMARY.

(Erase heading not required.)

Army Form C. 2118.

Hour, Date, Place	Summary of Events and Information	Remarks and references to Appendices
January 1916.		
1st	"C" platoon relieved "D" platoon on D.H.Q. Guard.	
3rd	1 Officer and 21 Other Ranks returned to the Coy from the Bombing School, LONGUEVILLETTE, all having passed as expert bombers.	
4th	Capt. M.H.R. Pakey, O.C. Coy. was evacuated to No.4 C.C.S. suffering from stuffiness and a growth of bone in the nose. Captain Godfrey W. Seys, second in command, assumed temporary command of the Company	
5th	The naming of Platoons was altered from letters A. to F. to numbers 1 to 6	
7th	The Coy. moved out from Outrebois at 9 a.m. arriving at Talmas at 12 noon.	

Army Form C. 2118.

WAR DIARY
or
INTELLIGENCE SUMMARY.
(Erase heading not required.)

Instructions regarding War Diaries and Intelligence Summaries are contained in F.S. Regs., Part II. and the Staff Manual respectively. Title pages will be prepared in manuscript.

Hour, Date, Place	Summary of Events and Information	Remarks and references to Appendices
January 1916.		
7 contd.	The journey was found very trying to the men, though only a distance of 14 miles. The roads were very heavy, with a head wind all the way, making the going, with fully loaded cycles, very hard. The billets at Talmas were poor but the comfort of the men was greatly added to by the substitution of a motor lorry for two G.S. waggons from the Train, i.e. the blanket & baggage waggons. This enabled all cooking utensils being brought along quickly, with the result that a hot meal was ready for the men soon after arrival.	
8.	The Coy left Talmas at 9 am and arrived at Daours at 11-30 am. The day was beautifully sunny and the roads good and the whole journey was carried out as smoothly as possible. The billets at Daours was good the whole Coy being accommodated in a drying loft of a Wool Mill beside the Canal. The motor lorry	

WAR DIARY
OR
INTELLIGENCE SUMMARY.

(Erase heading not required.)

Army Form C. 2118.

Hour, Date, Place	Summary of Events and Information	Remarks and references to Appendices
January, 1916		
8th contd.	lorry was again of the utmost use.	
12th	The Coy left DAOURS at 9 am and proceeding along the canal tow path arrived at ETINEHEM at 11.45 am after a splendid ride. Then the motor lorry after the unloading was returned to the Train. Billets in Etinehem were fair; straw was scarce, but a supply of this was required about the end of the month. An effort was also made to erect three tier bunks by means of stakes, wire netting and canvas, but these have been found very cold during the winter time.	
22nd	2nd Lt Browne and 2 other ranks went for a course at Vignacourt (Corps Hqrs) for the purpose of becoming Corps Observers.	

Army Form C. 2118.

WAR DIARY
or
INTELLIGENCE SUMMARY.
(Erase heading not required.)

Instructions regarding War Diaries and Intelligence Summaries are contained in F.S. Regs., Part II. and the Staff Manual respectively. Title pages will be prepared in manuscript.

Hour, Date, Place	Summary of Events and Information	Remarks and references to Appendices

January 1916.

26th. Capt. M.H.R. Oaty returned to the Coy from the Base.

28th. The Coy was ordered to "stand to" until further notice. 2nd Lt. O.H. Browne and 2 other ranks returned from Corps Headquarters having completed Observer's Course.

29th. After an application by Capt. Legg, Lt. Clarke were detailed to be attached from this date to the 15th Bn Manchester Regt for the purpose of Patrol duties on Vaux March. This order was however cancelled on the 25th and the Coy ordered to "stand to" as Mobile Divisional Reserve on account of the French on our right having lost Frise to the Germans.

During the month the following were added to the Mobilization Store:-

4 Lanterns, tent folding.

Army Form C. 2118.

WAR DIARY
or
INTELLIGENCE SUMMARY.
(Erase heading not required.)

Instructions regarding War Diaries and Intelligence Summaries are contained in F. S. Regs., Part II. and the Staff Manual respectively. Title pages will be prepared in manuscript.

Hour, Date, Place	Summary of Events and Information	Remarks and references to Appendices
January 1916.	The many advantages accruing from the addition of a motor lorry or light motor-van to the transport of the Coy. cannot be too strongly urged. Unlike Infantry the Coy moves quickly and is able to do far longer distances, and it is evident that when the Coy is performing its proper duty as advance screen to the Division in the Field, the cooking utensils would never reach in time to prepare any sort of a meal. Had a field cooker been provided this would perhaps have hardly overcome the difficulty, but a light motor lorry would be still better and the present system of dixie cooking be adhered to.

J. Begg | |

Army Form C. 2118.

WAR DIARY
or
INTELLIGENCE SUMMARY.
(Erase heading not required.)

Instructions regarding War Diaries and Intelligence Summaries are contained in F. S. Regs., Part II. and the Staff Manual respectively. Title pages will be prepared in manuscript.

Hour, Date, Place	Summary of Events and Information	Remarks and references to Appendices
	Supplement to December, 1915.	
	Three items of importance have not been noted in the Diary for the period of December	
(a)	On December 8th an issue of one extra blanket per man was authorized by G.H.Q. and for the purpose of transporting these one extra G.S. Waggon was to be supplied by the train for each move.	
(b)	From Decr 5th to 8th the Coy carried out under instructions from Divisional Headquarters the reconnaissance of some 8½ roads in the area W of the line BEAUMETZ - FIENVILLERS - CANDAS for the purpose of showing state of repair and possibilities for transport and the moving of troops	
(c)	On December 23rd C.S.M. Sherman was evacuated to a C.C.S. suffering from the effects of an old fracture of the shoulder.	

J. Snape.

30ᵗʰ Dist: Cychih
vol: 4

Confidential

War Diary

of

30th Divisional Cyclist Coy.

from 1st February, 1916 to 29th February, 1916

Volume 4.

Army Form C. 2118.

WAR DIARY
or
INTELLIGENCE SUMMARY.

(Erase heading not required.)

Instructions regarding War Diaries and Intelligence Summaries are contained in F. S. Regs., Part II. and the Staff Manual respectively. Title pages will be prepared in manuscript.

Hour, Date, Place	Summary of Events and Information	Remarks and references to Appendices
ETINEHEM	February 1916.	
1st	The Coy took over the charge of the Divisional Cycle Repair Shops and installed 1 N.C.O. and 3 men, trained Artificers.	
4th	Captain Seys and 25 Other Ranks proceeded to BRAY and there surrounded two mills, standing one mile to the S.E. of the town. The premises were duly searched and the inhabitants detained on suspicion of espionage.	
5th	Captain Seys proceeded to CHIPILLY for the purpose of making a report on the billetting & cellar capacity of the village.	
6th	Lt. Clarke carried out a survey of billetting & cellar capacity of the village of ETINEHEM.	
7th	2nd Lt. Scrutton drew up a plan for Divisional Headquarters of the existing defences around ETINEHEM.	

Army Form C. 2118.

WAR DIARY
or
INTELLIGENCE SUMMARY.
(Erase heading not required.)

Instructions regarding War Diaries and Intelligence Summaries are contained in F. S. Regs., Part II. and the Staff Manual respectively. Title pages will be prepared in manuscript.

Hour, Date, Place	Summary of Events and Information	Remarks and references to Appendices

ETINEHEM. February, 1916

9th Capt Seys, Lt Lee, 2nd Lt Scrutton + 8th Other Ranks drawn from Nos 4, 5 & 6 Platoons were detailed to be attached to the 2nd Bn Wiltshire Regt. for duty in the trenches. Capt Seys proceeded to CARNOY. 2nd Lt Scrutton + 40 other Ranks to trenches B.36-38. Lt Lee + 40 Other ranks remaining in BRAY in support

12th Lt Lee + party relieved 2nd Lt Scrutton + party in the trenches who returned to BRAY

14th Captain Seys returned to Coy at ETINEHEM

15th 2nd Lt Scrutton went to Casualty Clearing Station suffering from Bronchitis. 2nd Lt Ward took his place at BRAY

16th Captain Parry under orders from Divisional Headquarters handed over Command of the Coy to Capt Seys + proceeded to England

WAR DIARY
or
INTELLIGENCE SUMMARY.
(Erase heading not required.)

Army Form C. 2118.

Hour, Date, Place		Summary of Events and Information	Remarks and references to Appendices
ETINEHEM	February. 1916.		
	16th old	England to report to War Office. 2nd Lt Ward + party relieved Lt Lee + party in the trenches who returned to BRAY.	
	20th	Lt Lee + party relieved 2nd Lt Ward + party in the trenches who returned to BRAY.	
	21st	Lt Clarke + party of 38 other ranks drawn from Nos 1 + 2 Platoons	
	22nd	relieved 2nd Lt Ward + party at BRAY; the latter returned to ETINEHEM.	
	23rd	Lt. Grant + a party of 10 other ranks was detailed to fit name boards to all copses between CARNOY and SUZANNE.	
	24th	Lt. Clarke + party relieved Lt Lee + party in the trenches, the latter returning to BRAY.	
	25th	Lt. Grant and a party of 37 other ranks drawn from	
	26th	Nos 2 + 3 Platoons relieved Lt Lee + party at BRAY. the latter returned to ETINEHEM.	

WAR DIARY
or
INTELLIGENCE SUMMARY.
(Erase heading not required.)

Army Form C. 2118.

Hour, Date, Place	Summary of Events and Information	Remarks and references to Appendices
ETINEHEM February 1916. 26th	Lt Grant + party relieved Lt Clarke + party in the trenches the latter returning to BRAY. Lt Lee + No 6 Platoon took over the duties of Divisional Headquarter Guard	
28th	Both Lt Clarke + party + Lt Grant + party returned to the Coy at ETINEHEM, the 2nd Bn The Wiltshire Regt being relieved from the trenches. Additions to Mobilization Store table during the month :- N I L. During the month of February the Coy have been detailed to carry out various fatigues, amongst these the minding of a road running from ETINEHEM to Point 80 on the BRAY-CORBIE	

Army Form C. 2118.

WAR DIARY
or
INTELLIGENCE SUMMARY.
(Erase heading not required.)

Hour, Date, Place	Summary of Events and Information	Remarks and references to Appendices
February 1916.	Road. The demolition of the ETINEHEM windmill, (work abandoned before completed), and the clearing of ETINEHEM Roads generally. In addition to these and the work in trenches they have also carried on the following permanent duties:- Officers N.C.O. men A.P.M. Staff - 1 7 Corps Observers 1 2 2 Guard at ECLUSE Bridge - 1 4 Guard at Divisional H'dqrs 1 4 18 Signal Coy. Messengers - 4 7 Camp Commandants Staff 2 "G" Branch Orderlies 2 Two casualties occurred during the turn of the Coy. in the trenches 9546 Pte. Walton, J. - Shot hand through accidental discharge of his own rifle 9158 L/C McKellar, J. - Cut cheek from a stray bullet while going to trenches.	

J. S. Sayer (?) CAPTAIN,
COMMANDING 30TH DIVISIONAL CYCLIST COY.

30 Div Cyclists
Vol 5

Confidential

War Diary

of

30th Divisional Cyclist Coy

From 1st March, 1916 to 31st March 1916

Volume 5.

Army Form C. 2118.

WAR DIARY
or
INTELLIGENCE SUMMARY.

(Erase heading not required.)

Hour, Date, Place	Summary of Events and Information	Remarks and references to Appendices
March 1916		
1st to 14th	Nothing of any importance happened to the Coy during the remainder of our stay in ETINEHEM	
15th	The Coy moved out of the line to PONT NOYELLES	
16th	The Coy moved to QUERRIEUX and took over the duties of Railway Construction work on the railway being built from DAOURS through PONT NOYELLES	
21st	2nd Lt E.C Ruck joined the Coy for duty	
22nd	CAPT Seys left for England on to duty since LT CLARKE took over command of the Coy	
24th	No 108 Coy Sergt Major DALY joined the Coy for duty	
29th	The Coy moved into the Training Area taking up billets in LONGPRÉ	

Army Form C. 2118.

WAR DIARY
or
INTELLIGENCE SUMMARY.

(Erase heading not required.)

Hour, Date, Place	Summary of Events and Information	Remarks and references to Appendices
March 1916	Nil. The 30th Division completed its move out of the line on March 21st, moving back, and the relieving of our Brigade was finished. The 18th Division took the place of the 30th Division in the line.	
	Addition to Mobilization Stores during the month	
	Nil	

J.S. ___, CAPTAIN,
___

30 Div Cyclist
Vol 6

Confidential

War Diary

of

30th Divisional Cyclist Coy.

from 1st April, 1916 to 30th April 1916.

Volume 6.

WAR DIARY
or
INTELLIGENCE SUMMARY.

Army Form C. 2118.

(Erase heading not required.)

Hour, Date, Place	Summary of Events and Information	Remarks and references to Appendices
April 1916		
2nd	Captain Seys returned from Leave	
5th	The Coy in conjunction with the Divisional Cavalry (D Squadron Lancashire Hussars. Major Brownlow O.C.) and the 19th Motor Machine Gun Battery, carried out a training scheme "Vanguard to an advance guard of a Division on the March" under the supervision of Major General W. Fry C.B. the G.O.C. 30th Division.	
6th	Lt. Lee granted leave from 7th to 17th left for ENGLAND.	
9th	In conjunction with No. 1 & 3 Coy 30th Div. Train, the Coy organised a very successful day of sports which was well attended by Officers & men of the Division. The G.O.C. Division being present and judging several events.	
10th	Orders received for the Coy at full strength, to move into the training area of the 2nd Indian Cavalry Division and together with the 30th Divisional Cavalry and the 19th Motor Machine Gun Battery, to attached from the 13th to the AMBALA Brigade for 13 days training in open warfare.	

WAR DIARY
or
INTELLIGENCE SUMMARY.

(Erase heading not required.)

Army Form C. 2118.

Hour, Date, Place	Summary of Events and Information	Remarks and references to Appendices

April 1916.

11th — Lt Clarke and 1 Sergt granted Leave from 12th to 21st. Left for ENGLAND.

12th — The Coy moved out of LONGPRE at 9 am and arrived at HANGEST at 11.30 am, finding good billets.

13th — The Coy left HANGEST at 9 am and arrived at FRAMICOURT at 3 pm. Finding no billets there they moved to LETRANSLAY where good quarters were found and a meal prepared by 5.30 pm. The whole journey was very trying for Officers & men. This day was wet and the whole ride of 25 miles was against a fierce head wind and with a preponderance of uphill all the way.

14th — Under instructions from the AMBALA Brigade the Coy moved from LETRANSLAY to the small village of WATTERBLERIE some 3 miles away. This was effected by about noon & the rest of the day spent in cleaning up.

15th — Scheme "Advance and Flank Guard to a Convoy" postponed owing to rain.

16th — All leave stopped and all ranks to be recalled by the 18th.

17th — Scheme as above carried out under Col. Lane, 30th Lancers.

Army Form C. 2118.

WAR DIARY
or
INTELLIGENCE SUMMARY.
(Erase heading not required.)

Instructions regarding War Diaries and Intelligence Summaries are contained in F.S. Regs., Part II. and the Staff Manual respectively. Title pages will be prepared in manuscript.

Hour, Date, Place	Summary of Events and Information	Remarks and references to Appendices
April 1916:		
18th	Scheme "Vanguard to Infantry Advance Guard" cancelled owing to rain. Lt Clarke, Lt Lee and 1 Sergt returned from Leave.	
20th	Scheme "Taking up a Defensive Position" carried out under Major Mort, 8th Hussars.	
24th	Brigade Day - Scheme "Covering the Concentration of the AMBALA Brigade" Major Mort, 90 & 8th Hussars together with the 30th Div Mounted Troops & the 19th MMG, carried out the scheme. The day concluded with a march past in column of route before the G.O.C. 2nd Indian Cavalry and Lord Birnie, G.O.C. AMBALA Brigade.	
25th	Scheme "Vanguard to an Advance Guard of a Division on the March" under Major Bromilow. D Squadron Lord Strivar (30th Div Mounted Troops) was posted out under the supervision of the GOC AMBALA Brigade. The Coy moved back out of the Cavalry Training Area.	
26th	Starting at 9 a.m. they arrived at HANGEST at 12 noon after a very hot dusty ride. The Coy occupied the same good billets	

Army Form C. 2118.

WAR DIARY
or
INTELLIGENCE SUMMARY.
(Erase heading not required.)

Hour, Date, Place	Summary of Events and Information	Remarks and references to Appendices
April 1916		
27th	The Coy. left HANGEST at 10 a.m. and proceeding along the canal tow-path arrived at LONGPRE at 12 noon. 30th Divisional Operation Orders No 13 were here received giving the details of the move of the Division back into the line. The Cyclist Coy to start on the 3rd and arrive at ETINEHEM on the 4th.	
28th	Leave again opened for the Coy. Increase in Mobilization from NIL during the Month. The Coy received 4 men as drafts to replace men sent to the Base for various reasons.	

J S Benyon CAPTAIN,
COMMANDING 30TH DIVISIONAL CYCLIST COY.

30 Div
Cyclists
Vol 7

Confidential

War Diary

of

30th Divisional Cyclist Coy

from 1st May 1916 to 22nd May 1916

Volume 7.

WAR DIARY
or
INTELLIGENCE SUMMARY.
(Erase heading not required.)

Army Form C. 2118.

Instructions regarding War Diaries and Intelligence Summaries are contained in F.S. Regs., Part II and the Staff Manual respectively. Title pages will be prepared in manuscript.

Hour, Date, Place	Summary of Events and Information	Remarks and references to Appendices
May 1916.		
1st	The allotment of leave for the Coy was increased from 2 to 3 every 5 days.	
3rd	The Coy. left LONGPRE at 9 am & arrived at CORBIE at 2.30 pm. The delay was due to a muddle over the billeting which was not however the fault of anyone in the Coy. The billets were foot.	
4th	Starting at 11 am the Coy. arrived at ETINEHEM at 1 pm after a good ride along the Canal towpath. The same billets as before were allotted to the Coy. & these were found much improved having been turned out by the Cyclist Coy, 164 Division.	
5th	The 30th Division completed its move into the line — The report on the recent training under the 2nd Indian Cavalry Division was received, in which the following paragraph appeared "The 19th Motor Machine Gun Battery & the 30th . 36th Cyclist Coy are efficient units but require more work with other troops".	
8th	Orders received that it has been decided to remove Cyclist Coy. & Cavalry Squadrons from Divisions & form them into Battalions & Regiments under Corps control. 30th & 18th Cyclist Coy with one another not yet detailed to be attached to XIII Corps.	

WAR DIARY
or
INTELLIGENCE SUMMARY.

(Erase heading not required.)

Army Form C. 2118.

Hour, Date, Place	Summary of Events and Information	Remarks and references to Appendices
May 1916		
8th south	XIII Corps. Date of move to be notified later.	
17th	Orders received for Capt. Step to attend at Corps H.Q. where he was instructed to carry out the re-organisation of the 18th & 30th Divl Coys into the XIII Corps Cyclist Battalion.	
21st	The Coy. moved from ETINEHEM at 9 a.m. & concentrated at VAUX sur SOMME with the 18th Divl Coy.	
22nd	Personnel & properties of the Coy. were transferred as follows under Q.H.Q. No OB 1517. To XIII Corps Cyclist Battalion 8 Officers, 154 Other Ranks + all property. To 3rd Infantry Base Depot 5 Other Ranks as 1st Reserve. To 2nd Bn Royal Scots Fusiliers 33 Other Ranks. Totals - 8 Officers, 192 Other Ranks.	
	Note: The Coy. was one under strength at the time.	

Signed
CAPTAIN,
COMMANDING 30TH DIVISIONAL CYCLIST COY.